Finar Trading Patterns

Tony Loton

LOTONtech

www.lotontech.com

Contents

Acknowledgements

I'd like to thank all those who volunteered to review the original manuscript for this book; for no more reward than a mention here – and a free copy.

I'd also like to thank my family, for humoring me while I'm "not doing a normal job".

About the author

Tony Loton has traded various financial instruments on his own account since the turn of the millennium, including: stocks, funds, exchange-traded funds, covered warrants and listed contracts for difference. These days most of his trading activity is directed towards financial spread trading (aka. spread betting).

Tony has previously written and published the book "DON'T LOSE MONEY! (in the Stock Markets)" as a well as a series of IT books with a stock trading bias.

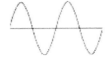

0 – About Financial Trading Patterns

Are you wondering why I've numbered this first chapter '0', rather than '1'?

It's because in this chapter I want to introduce the idea of financial trading patterns, and explain how they are presented in this book; and I want the first real pattern that I present (LIMIT BUY) to be numbered '1', which leaves '0' for this chapter's number.

I could have labeled this chapter simply 'Introduction', but then I fear you would simply skip over to the body of the book. Believe it or not, for many years I consistently ignored the 'Introduction' of each book that I read... so keen, was I, to cut to the chase.

If you've read this far I conclude that you're not an introduction-skipper; which is good, because what I tell you here will be invaluable in your understanding of the rest of the book.

About Financial Trading Patterns

If you're expecting this book to contain the technical analysis chart patterns that you see in other trading books, you'll be disappointed; or maybe pleasantly surprised. You won't find any cups-with-handles, candlesticks, head-and-shoulders, or double bottoms here. You will find 'financial trading patterns', which is the term I use to describe patterns of trading activity that you can apply to enact your trading strategy.

If you bought a book on knitting patterns, you wouldn't expect it to contain patterns for you to spot in people's knitwear as you walk the streets; you'd expect it to contain patterns in the form of recipes that you can apply – and combine – to achieve your knitting objectives. If you bought a book on software engineering 'design patterns', you would see the patterns described generically as follows:

"Software patterns are reusable solutions to recurring problems that occur during software development."

– Mark Grand, Patterns in Java (Volume 1), Wiley, 1998.

I'll adapt that definition, and use it to define my term 'financial trading patterns' as follows:

"Financial trading patterns are reusable solutions to recurring problems that occur during financial trading."

– Tony Loton, 2007

The problems at which these patterns are targeted include:

- The problem of how to buy low, sell high

- The problem of how to buy high, sell higher (for momentum traders)

- The problem of how to cut your losses, and let your profits run

Why 'financial' trading patterns?
My original idea was to name this book simply 'trading patterns', but my fear was that some people would buy the book expecting it to teach them how to 'trade' on eBay.

Maybe I've missed a trick there as it would certainly generate more sales!

My next idea was to name the book 'stock trading patterns'. That would be more accurate, but might have fooled you in to thinking that the patterns may only be applied to individual stocks or equities.

The fact is that these patterns may be applied to a range of financial instruments including equities, indexes, currencies, and spread bets; as long as your broker provides one or more order types on those instruments including: limit orders, stop orders, and trailing stop orders. Where I use words such as 'stock' for simplicity (as in "If the stock price rises...") do keep in mind the fact that I might also mean any of the other tradable financial instruments or securities.

There are some subtleties. For example your broker will most likely allow you to apply the patterns to indexes traded as Exchange Traded Funds (ETFs) but not to indexes traded as traditional mutual funds. Your spread trading provider might allow you to trade 'short' versions of these patterns, by inverting them, and thereby benefitting from falling prices; but your regular stockbroker might not.

Technical Trading vs. Value Investing

You might think that these patterns are aimed squarely at technical traders who follow price action. Yes; the patterns are certainly useful to technical traders, but are not exclusively aimed at them. Remember that these patterns show you how to achieve various trading objectives by combining stockbroker order types. I do not necessarily mandate *when* the patterns should be applied.

As an illustration, consider the LIMIT BUY pattern which has the objective of 'buying low'. A technical trader may conclude that a stock price is about to reach a low point because she has observed a 'double bottom' formation. A value investor might assess company fundamentals to determine at what price a stock would be considered 'good value', and place a LIMIT BUY order to buy in automatically at that price. Both types will be interested in *Chapter 1 – LIMIT BUY*.

Even the most die-hard 'buy and hold' investor would be wise to set a STOP SELL order at some point, say minus 20%, so as to sell out in the event of a major catastrophe. He will be interested in *Chapter 5 – STOP SELL*.

Anatomy of a pattern
The patterns are presented in a standardized format, each one comprising a **name, definitions, parameters, objective, motivation, success scenario(s), failure scenario(s)**, and **application**.

Name
This is the concise name that I have given to the pattern. A concise name allows one pattern to be referenced easily by another pattern, and provides a shorthand nomenclature for traders to use when discussing the patterns.

Where possible I have based the names of the simpler patterns on the names of the stockbroker order types that are already in common usage. When combining patterns, I have combined the names of the order types to give pattern names such as LIMIT BUY, LIMIT SELL. Not only does that aid in their application, but it also ensures that each pattern name is unique.

The LIMIT BUY, LIMIT SELL pattern might just as well have been named the BUY LOW, SELL HIGH pattern. But the latter name could apply just as well to the STOP BUY, STOP SELL pattern.

Definitions
This is a set of one or more formal definitions for the order type(s) utilized in the pattern.

Parameters
The parameters are the values that you can vary when applying the pattern. While the shape of a pattern is fixed, its dimensions may be varied by adjusting the parameters. You can see that pictorially in (A) and (B) of Figure 1 below.

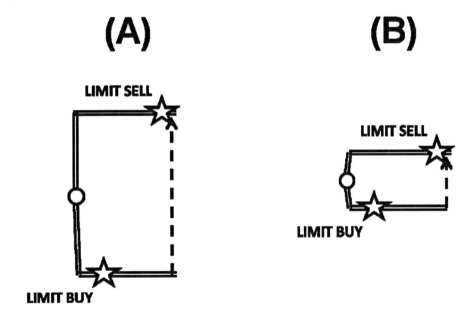

Figure 1 LIMIT BUY, LIMIT SELL with different parameter values

This section merely lists the parameters of the pattern. It does not attempt to suggest effective values for the parameters. You will find some suggestions in chapter *13 –*

Author's use of Trading Patterns, but if I knew the definitive answers I would be a lot richer than I am.

Objective

This is a summary of the problem that the pattern aims to solve. For example, "to solve the problem of how to buy low, sell high."

The objective and the motivation (below) help to resolve the pattern naming issue. Several patterns may share an objective while having different (unique) names.

Motivation

This is the reason for the pattern's existence.

In some cases the motivation is cumulative, because each pattern that answers a question ("how to?") might at the same time raise further questions ("what if?"). In those cases it is possible for a later pattern to be motivated to provide a "how to?" answer to an earlier patterns "what if?" consequential questions.

Success Scenario(s)

The success scenario(s) describe one or more situations in which applying a pattern achieves the intended end result; i.e. it works out as planned.

The success scenario is presented in an easy-to-read pictorial format like this:

Financial Trading Patterns

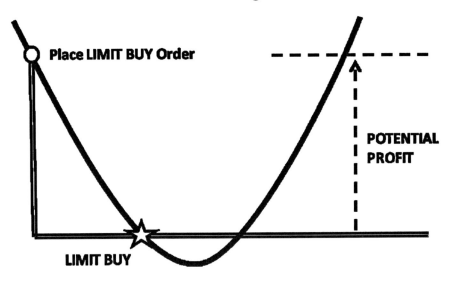

Figure 2 SAMPLE success scenario

In many cases a pattern will have one single significant success scenario, but it is possible for there to be more than one.

Failure Scenario(s)

The failure scenario(s) describe one or more situations in which applying a pattern fails to achieve the intended end result; i.e. it does not work out as planned.

Each failure scenario is presented in an easy-to-read pictorial format like this:

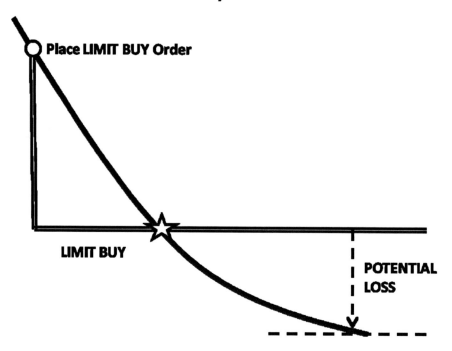

Figure 3 SAMPLE failure scenario

In general there will be more failure scenarios than success scenarios for a given pattern. It's a fact of life that things can go wrong in more ways than they can go right.

Often there will be two failure scenarios for a given pattern: one that results in a loss, and one that results in a failure to realize a profit.

Application
This is a description of how the pattern could be applied in practice, using the appropriate stockbroker order types; with mention of any special conditions that your stockbroker might apply.

Key to symbols

Look back at the SAMPLE scenarios shown in Figure 2 and Figure 3. The symbols used in those figures – and in the rest of the book – are as follows.

The ○ symbol represents an order being placed to deal automatically when a particular condition occurs: e.g. when the price rises to a particular value or falls to a particular value.

The ☆ symbol represents a deal being done immediately at the current market price. This would either be automatic, as a result of a previously placed order being executed; or manual because we instruct the stockbroker at that point to deal (buy or sell) 'at best'.

The wavy line (〜) represents the fluctuating price of the stock or other financial instrument. These lines are stylized; which is to say that the simplest possible arc, sine wave, or other curve is used to imply particular price behavior.

The double line (⌐   ) which is generally an L shape, or inverted L shape, connects an order (○) with the point-in-time at which it is executed (☆). It shows the amount by which a price must rise or fall in order to trigger execution. An order is executed only if or when the double line is intersected by the price line (〜).

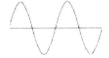

1 – LIMIT BUY

NAME
LIMIT BUY

DEFINITIONS
A LIMIT BUY order is an order to BUY a security when the price falls to a specified level.

PARAMETERS
LIMIT BUY Trigger Price.

OBJECTIVE
The objective is to buy a stock when it's cheap.

MOTIVATION
We'd like to buy low and sell high. This pattern satisfies the 'buy low' condition.

SUCCESS SCENARIO(s)
Figure 4 shows the LIMIT BUY success scenario.

When the price is high we place a LIMIT BUY order ○ to purchase the stock when the price falls to what we consider to be good value. Shortly after the order executes ☆, the price rises and we have a potential profit.

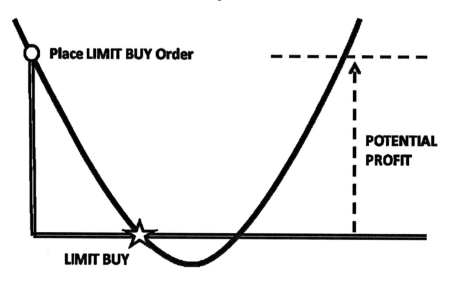

Figure 4 LIMIT BUY success scenario

Notionally we have profited by the difference between: the LIMIT BUY PRICE, and the higher price at which we placed the order rather than simply buying then.

The profit that we actually realize may be more or less, depending on when we decide to sell.

FAILURE SCENARIO(s)

Figure 5 shows the most obvious failure scenario, in which the price continues to fall after the LIMIT BUY order has executed. We stand to make a loss, the size of which depends on when we decide to sell out; or we can hold out for a subsequent rise, all the while showing a 'paper loss'.

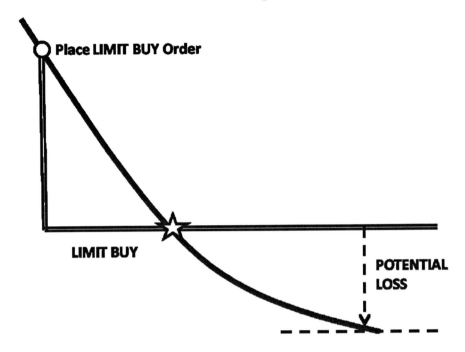

Figure 5 LIMIT BUY failure scenario

This is not the only failure scenario. Another failure scenario is the one in which the price does not fall at all after we place the LIMIT BUY order. The prices rises, we never buy in, and we fail to benefit from any profit potential.

APPLICATION

Your stockbroker should offer a LIMIT BUY order type, which executes when the price falls to a specified level.

You specify a level to which you wish the price to fall before the order executes.

Note that you must place a LIMIT BUY order when the current price is above the price at which you wish to buy, otherwise the order will execute immediately at the current price.

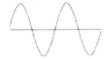

2 – LIMIT SELL

NAME
LIMIT SELL

DEFINITIONS
A LIMIT SELL order is an order to SELL a security when the price rises to a specified level.

PARAMETERS
LIMIT SELL Trigger Price.

OBJECTIVE
The objective is to bank a profit.

MOTIVATION
We'd like to buy low and sell high. This pattern satisfies the 'sell high' condition.

SUCCESS SCENARIO(s)
Figure 6 shows the LIMIT BUY success scenario.

We buy a rising stock and place a LIMIT SELL order o to sell the stock when the price rises to what we consider to be a healthy profit. When the order executes ☆, we bank the profit.

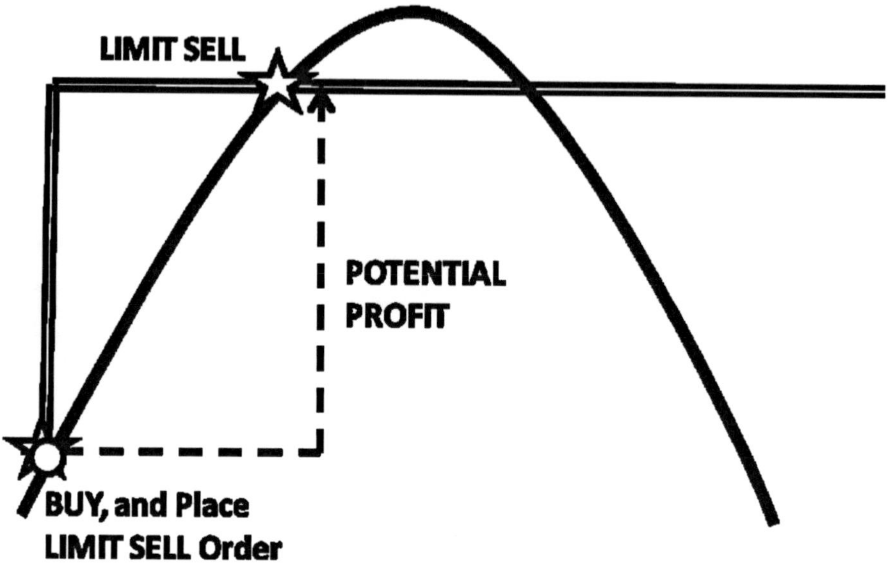

Figure 6 LIMIT SELL success scenario

FAILURE SCENARIO(s)

Figure 7 shows the most obvious failure scenario, in which the price continues to rise after the order executes. There is additional potential profit, which we fail to realize by selling out too soon.

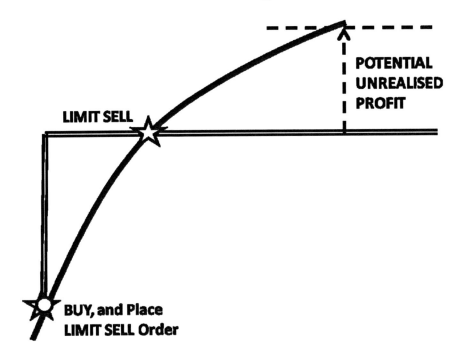

POTENTIAL
UNREALISED
PROFIT

LIMIT SELL

BUY, and Place
LIMIT SELL Order

Figure 7 LIMIT SELL failure scenario

That's not the only failure scenario. Another failure scenario is the one in which the price does not continue to rise after we buy the stock initially, but it falls instead. In that case we stand to make a loss.

APPLICATION

Your stockbroker should offer a LIMIT SELL order type, which executes when the price rises to a specified level.

You specify a level to which you wish the price to rise before the order executes.

Note that you must place a LIMIT SELL order when the current price is below the price at which you wish to sell, otherwise the order could potentially execute immediately at the current price. I say 'potentially' because some stockbroker accounts will allow you to sell a particular security only if you currently own that security.

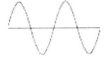

3 – LIMIT BUY, LIMIT SELL

NAME
LIMIT BUY, LIMIT SELL

DEFINITIONS
A LIMIT BUY order is an order to BUY a security when the price falls to a specified level.

A LIMIT SELL order is an order to SELL a security when the price rises to a specified level.

PARAMETERS
LIMIT BUY Trigger Price.

LIMIT SELL Trigger Price.

OBJECTIVE
The objective is to buy low, sell high.

MOTIVATION
We'd like to buy low and sell high. This pattern satisfies both conditions.

SUCCESS SCENARIO(s)
Figure 8 shows the LIMIT BUY, LIMIT SELL success scenario.

After witnessing several peaks and troughs, we identify what we consider to be a stock's trading range. We place a LIMIT BUY order to buy-in near the bottom of the trading range, and a LIMIT SELL order to sell out near the top of the trading range.

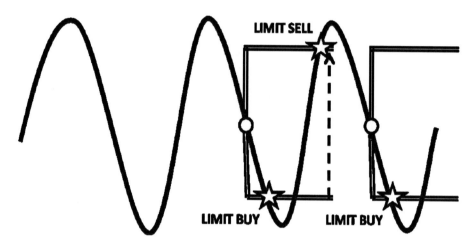

Figure 8 LIMIT BUY, LIMIT SELL success scenario

If all goes according to plan, our profit is the difference between the LIMIT BUY and LIMIT SELL prices. We can repeat the pattern as long as the stock price continues to oscillate within the trading range.

A note for value investors
A described in this scenario, we set the LIMIT BUY and LIMIT SELL trigger prices based on technical factors; i.e. a trading range that we had identified by looking at the price history. Alternatively, from a value investing point of view, we could set the LIMIT BUY and LIMIT SELL trigger prices according to what we consider to be undervalued and overvalued price levels for the security in question.

FAILURE SCENARIO(s)
There are several possible failure scenarios for this pattern as follows:

- The trading range breaks down and the price continues to fall after the LIMIT BUY executes, resulting in a 'paper' loss.

- The trading range breaks down and the price continues to rise after the LIMIT SELL executes, resulting in unrealized profits.

- The trading range narrows, so the orders do not execute.

APPLICATION

You implement this pattern using your stockbroker's LIMIT BUY and LIMIT SELL order types.

For each order, you specify a price at which you wish the order to execute.

You may or may not be able to place both orders simultaneously in the manner shown in Figure 8. I can apply the pattern in that way via my spread trading account, which places no restrictions on such set-ups. I cannot do that via my regular stockbroker account, which allows me to place a LIMIT SELL order only on a stock that I actually hold – i.e. after the LIMIT BUY order has executed.

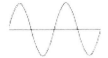

4 – STOP BUY

NAME
STOP BUY

DEFINITIONS
A STOP BUY order is an order to BUY a security when the price rises to a specified level.

PARAMETERS
STOP BUY Trigger Price.

OBJECTIVE
The objective is to buy a rising stock.

MOTIVATION
Momentum traders believe that a rising stock will continue to rise, to the extent that it is even possible to 'buy high, sell higher'.

Alternatively, as expressed in the following scenario, the STOP BUY pattern allows you to 'buy low' as with LIMIT BUY, but without the potential loss.

SUCCESS SCENARIO(s)
Figure 9 shows the STOP BUY success scenario.

When we think the stock price has stopped falling, and is about to rise, we place a STOP BUY order to buy the stock if it does indeed rise to a specified level.

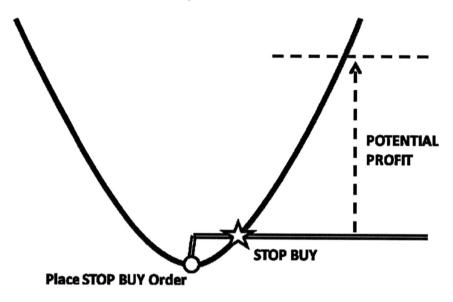

Figure 9 STOP BUY success scenario

If the price continues to rise after the STOP BUY order has executed, we have a potential profit.

You will recognize this scenario as similar to the LIMIT BUY scenario; but there's one important difference. If the price falls immediately after we place the STOP BUY order, the order does not execute and we do not stand to make a loss.

A note for value investors

In this scenario we decided to place our STOP BUY order purely in response to a technical indicator, i.e. the price trend appeared to reverse. Value investors might place the STOP BUY order when they consider the security in question to be undervalued, using the price trend reversal merely for confirmation.

FAILURE SCENARIO(s)

Figure 10 shows the most obvious failure scenario, in which the trend reverses and the price falls after the STOP BUY executes. This results in a potential loss.

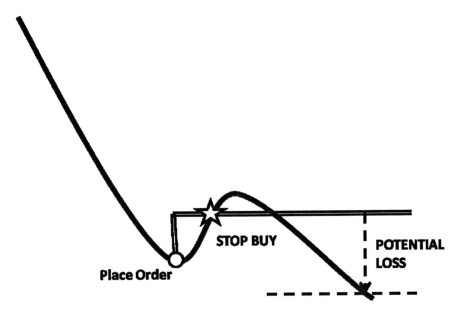

Figure 10 STOP BUY failure scenario

That's not the only failure scenario. Another failure scenario is the one in which the price does not rise, but falls after we place the STOP BUY order. We do not make a loss, but we fail to realize additional profit if the price does eventually recover from a new low point up to our STOP BUY point.

APPLICATION

Your stockbroker should offer a STOP BUY order type, which executes when the price rises to a specified level.

You specify a level to which you want the price to rise before the order executes.

Note that you must place a STOP BUY order when the current price is below the price at which you wish to buy, otherwise the order will execute immediately at the current price.

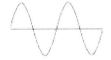

5 – STOP SELL

NAME
STOP SELL

DEFINITIONS
A STOP SELL order is an order to SELL a security when the price falls to a specified level.

PARAMETERS
STOP SELL Trigger Price.

OBJECTIVE
The objective is to stop a loss, or secure a profit.

MOTIVATION
The first objective is to stop a loss, which is really how the STOP order – commonly known as the STOP LOSS order – got its name. Although financial traders disagree on many things, most agree that we should strive to 'cut losses'.

The second objective is to secure a profit when our stock has risen in price, but not to limit our profit potential in the way that LIMIT SELL does.

SUCCESS SCENARIO(s)
Figure 11 shows the success scenario in which the STOP SELL helps us to stop a loss.

As soon as we buy a stock that we think is rising, we place a STOP SELL at some price below the current price; which represents our acceptable loss. This price stops rising, it falls, and breaches the STOP SELL price thus protecting us from further falls.

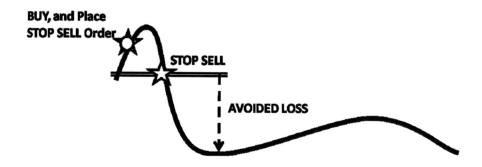

Figure 11 STOP SELL success scenario (stop loss)

Figure 12 shows the success scenario in which the STOP SELL helps us to secure a profit.

Once our stock purchase has risen in price to show a healthy profit, we set a STOP SELL below the current price; thus securing most of the profit if the price begins to fall.

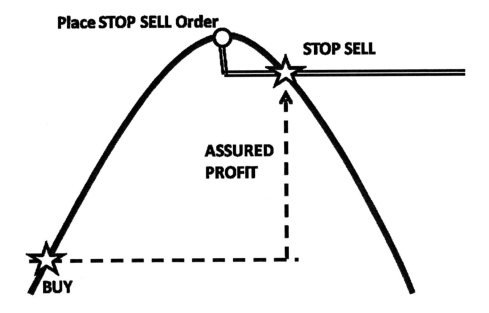

Figure 12 STOP SELL success scenario (secure profit)

In this scenario, if the price continues to rise, the STOP SELL will not execute and we could gain yet more profit.

A note for value investors

In this scenario we decided to place our STOP SELL order purely in response to a technical indicator, i.e. the price trend appeared to reverse. Value investors might place the STOP SELL order when they consider the security in question to be overvalued, using the price trend reversal merely for confirmation.

FAILURE SCENARIO(s)

A not-so-obvious failure scenario is the one in which the price behaves as just described – i.e. continues to rise – but then falls back to our STOP SELL level and we fail to capture any of the additional profit. This problem will be addressed using a TRAILING STOP, described later.

Figure 13 shows the more obvious failure scenario, in which the prices falls (triggering our STOP SELL) then promptly rises when we no longer hold the stock.

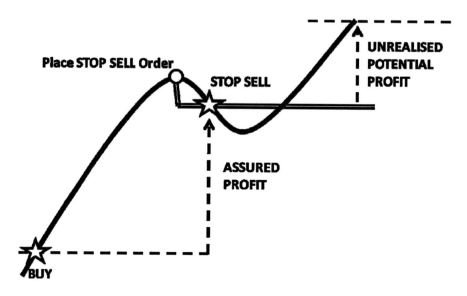

Figure 13 STOP SELL failure scenario

APPLICATION

Your stockbroker should offer a STOP SELL order type, which executes when the price falls to a specified level.

You specify a level to which you want the price to fall before the order executes.

Note that you must place a STOP SELL order when the current price is above the price at which you wish to sell, otherwise the order will execute immediately at the current price.

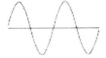

6 – STOP BUY, STOP SELL

NAME
STOP BUY, STOP SELL

DEFINITIONS
A STOP BUY order is an order to BUY a security when the price rises to a specified level.

A STOP SELL order is an order to SELL a security when the price falls to a specified level.

PARAMETERS
STOP BUY Trigger Price.

STOP SELL Trigger Price.

OBJECTIVE
The objective is to buy at the onset of an uptrend, sell on a downtrend.

MOTIVATION
This pattern could be used for the same reason as the LIMIT BUY, LIMIT SELL pattern; to buy low and sell high. By using STOP orders rather than LIMIT orders we benefit because:

- We buy when the price is rising, and therefore more likely to continue rising.

- We only sell when the price starts to fall, not when it reaches an arbitrary level below the true profit potential.

This pattern might also be used for momentum trading. That is: buy a rising stock high, sell it even higher.

SUCCESS SCENARIO(s)

Figure 14 shows two success scenarios in one:

- In the first scenario we observe a trading range. At the bottom of the range we **Place a STOP BUY Order**, which is executed on the upturn. At the top of the range we **Place a STOP SELL Order**, which is executed on the downturn; thus securing a profit.

- In the second scenario, we observe that the price is at a low point. We **Place a STOP BUY Order**, which is executed on the upturn. When we think the trend is reversing we **Place a STOP SELL Order**, which is not executed because the uptrend re-establishes. The price rises considerably and at the next anticipated trend reversal we **Place a STOP SELL Order**; which is executed, thus securing a profit.

Figure 14 STOP BUY, STOP SELL success scenario

In the second success scenario you will have noticed that we placed two STOP SELL orders in succession, the second one at a higher level. In effect we've used a TRAILING STOP, which is the next pattern that we'll consider.

A note for value investors

As suggested in the scenarios discussions of the separate STOP BUY and STOP SELL patterns, value investors might use the price trend reversals merely as confirmations to support their hypotheses that the security in question is overvalued or undervalued at the times that the orders are placed.

FAILURE SCENARIO(s)

There are several possible failure scenarios, combining the failure scenarios for the separate STOP BUY and STOP SELL patterns presented earlier. Some of the failure scenarios are as follows:

- The trend might reverse immediately after our STOP BUY triggers, taking us into loss.

- The trend might reverse after triggering our STOP SELL, so that that we miss out on further profit potential.

- When we set a STOP BUY, the price might fall significantly, rather than rising and triggering our order. If the price subsequently rises all the way back up to our STOP BUY level, we buy-in having missed the additional profit potential of the fall-and-rise.

- When we set the STOP SELL, the price might rise significantly, rather than falling and triggering our order. If the price subsequently falls all the way back down to our STOP SELL level, we sell-out having missed the additional profit potential of the rise-and-fall.

The first two failure scenarios result in whipsaw losses, which can be minimized by setting stop orders at an appropriate distance from the current price.

The second two failure scenarios can be mitigated through the use of TRAILING STOP orders, discussed next.

APPLICATION
You implement this pattern using your stockbroker's STOP BUY and STOP SELL order types.

For each order, you specify a price at which you wish the order to execute.

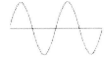

7 – TRAILING STOP BUY

NAME
TRAILING STOP BUY

DEFINITIONS
A TRAILING STOP BUY order is an order to BUY a security when the price rises by a specified amount above the prevailing market price. A TRAILING STOP BUY tracks a falling price.

PARAMETERS
STOP BUY Trigger Distance.

OBJECTIVE
The objective is to buy on an uptrend, at a low price.

MOTIVATION
One of the failure scenarios for the STOP BUY, STOP SELL pattern was as follows:

- When we set a STOP BUY above the current price, the price might fall significantly, not triggering our order. If the price subsequently rises all the way back up to our STOP BUY level, we buy-in having missed the additional profit potential of the fall-and-rise.

In other words: although we have bought at the onset of an uptrend, we have bought at a higher price than necessary.

SUCCESS SCENARIO

Figure 15 shows the success scenario in which the TRAILING STOP BUY helps us to buy on an uptrend, at a low price.

With the price trending down, we place a TRAILING STOP BUY order with a trigger price above the current price. As the price falls, the TRAILING STOP is adjusted downwards at the same rate. At some point the trend reverses sufficiently to trigger the STOP BUY order.

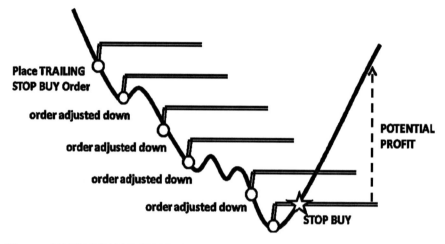

Figure 15 TRAILING STOP BUY success scenario

The advantage of this pattern is that we don't need to guess when we might be at the end of a downtrend, beginning of an uptrend. The TRAILING STOP order tracks the price down until the trend reverses from its lowest point.

A note for value investors
This pattern is more technical in nature than the earlier ones. The decision to buy-in is determined (automatically) according to the price action, rather than by any notion of the security being undervalued in absolute terms at that point.

FAILURE SCENARIO(s)

Figure 16 shows the most obvious failure scenario, in which the price falls dramatically soon after our TRAILING STOP BUY has executed.

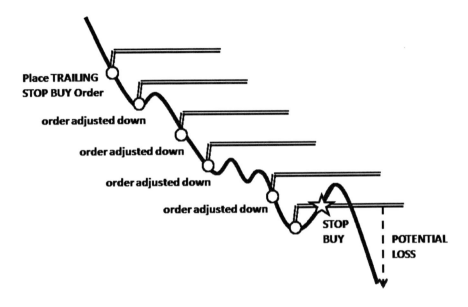

Figure 16 TRAILING STOP BUY failure scenario

Although we stand to make a loss in that scenario, at least we bought-in at what we consider to be a low price.

Another failure scenario is the one in which our STOP BUY order executes at the original trigger price soon after we place it, without having fallen first, and then the price falls dramatically.

APPLICATION

Ideally you would implement this pattern using your stockbroker's TRAILING STOP BUY order type.

You specify an amount by which you want the price to rise before the order executes.

If your stockbroker does not offer trailing stops, you can still trail the stops yourself by adjusting the trigger price of your non-trailing STOP order periodically, in line with the changing stock price.

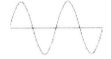

8 – TRAILING STOP SELL

NAME
TRAILING STOP SELL

DEFINITIONS
A TRAILING STOP SELL order is an order to SELL a security when the price falls by a specified amount below the prevailing market price. A TRAILING STOP SELL tracks a rising price.

PARAMETERS
STOP SELL Trigger Distance.

OBJECTIVE
The objective is to sell at the onset of a downtrend, at a high price.

MOTIVATION
One of the failure scenarios for the STOP BUY, STOP SELL pattern was as follows:

- When we set a STOP SELL below the current price, the price might rise significantly, not triggering our order. If the price subsequently falls all the way back up to our STOP SELL level, we sell-out having missed the additional profit potential of the rise-and-fall.

In other words: although we have sold on a downtrend, we have sold at a lower price than necessary.

SUCCESS SCENARIO(s)

Figure 17 shows the success scenario in which the TRAILING STOP SELL helps us to sell on a downtrend, at a high price.

With the price trending up, we place a TRAILING STOP SELL order with a trigger price below the current price. As the price rises, the TRAILING STOP is adjusted upwards at the same rate. At some point the trend reverses sufficiently to trigger the STOP SELL.

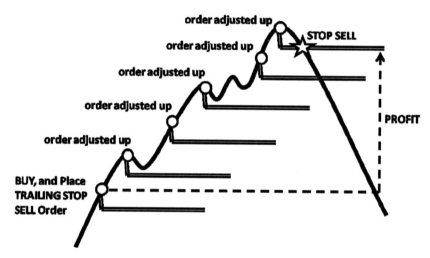

Figure 17 TRAILING STOP SELL success scenario

You might remember that we did something similar in chapter **6 – STOP BUY, STOP SELL**, but at that point we didn't call it a TRAILING STOP. Technically it wasn't a trailing stop because we placed a second STOP SELL order at the higher price, rather than adjusting the original order upwards.

A note for value investors
As with the TRAILING STOP BUY pattern, this pattern is more technical in nature than the earlier ones. The decision to sell-out is determined (automatically) according to the price

action, rather than by any notion of the security being overvalued in absolute terms at that point.

FAILURE SCENARIO(s)

The failure scenarios for this pattern are the exact mirrors of those for the TRAILING STOP BUY. That is...

- The price rises dramatically soon after the STOP SELL order executes, so we sold out too soon.

- The STOP SELL order executes at the original trigger price soon after we place it, without rising first, and then the price rises dramatically.

APPLICATION

Ideally you would implement this pattern using your stockbroker's TRAILING STOP SELL order type.

You specify an amount by which you want the price to fall before the order executes.

If your stockbroker does not offer trailing stops, you can still trail the stops yourself by adjusting the trigger price of your STOP order periodically, in line with the changing stock price.

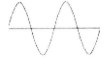

9 – TRAILING STOP BUY, TRAILING STOP SELL

NAME
TRAILING STOP BUY, TRAILING STOP SELL

DEFINITIONS
A TRAILING STOP BUY order is an order to BUY a security when the price rises by a specified amount above the market price. A TRAILING STOP BUY tracks a falling price.

A TRAILING STOP SELL order is an order to SELL a security when the price falls by a specified amount below the prevailing market price. A TRAILING STOP SELL tracks a rising price.

PARAMETERS
STOP BUY Trigger Distance.

STOP SELL Trigger Distance.

OBJECTIVE
The objective is to buy at the onset of an uptrend, at a low price; sell at the onset of a downtrend at a high price.

MOTIVATION
In effect this pattern combines two motivations, which are:

- to buy low, sell high

- to buy or sell in line with the trend

Thus we have an opportunity to realize maximum profit potential in rising and falling markets.

SUCCESS SCENARIO(s)

Figure 18 shows the success scenario in which the TRAILING STOP BUY helps us to buy at the onset of an uptrend, at a low price; and the TRAILING STOP SELL helps us to sell at the onset of a downtrend, at a high price.

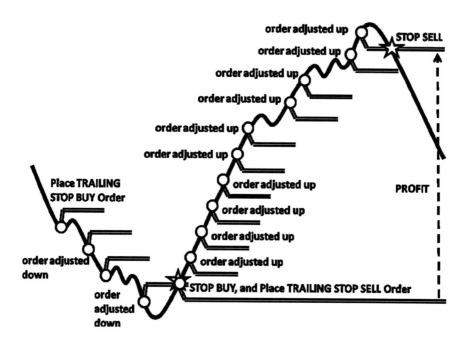

Figure 18 TRAILING STOP BUY, TRAILING STOP SELL success scenario

FAILURE SCENARIO(s)

The failure scenarios for this pattern occur when the price trend reverses soon after one or other of the orders executes. For example; if the price falls soon after the TRAILING STOP BUY executes, or the price rises soon after the TRAILING STOP SELL executes.

APPLICATION

Ideally you would implement this pattern using your stockbroker's TRAILING STOP BUY and TRAILING STOP SELL order types.

For the TRAILING STOP BUY, you specify an amount by which you want the price to rise before the order executes.

For the TRAILING STOP SELL, you specify an amount by which you want the price to fall before the order executes.

If your stockbroker does not offer trailing stops, you can still trail the stops yourself by adjusting the trigger price of your STOP order periodically, in line with the changing stock price.

10 – STOP/LIMIT

NAME
STOP/LIMIT

DEFINITIONS
A STOP/LIMIT BUY order is an order to BUY a security when the price rises to a specified (STOP) level, providing the price has not risen above a second (LIMIT) level.

A STOP/LIMIT SELL order is an order to SELL a security when the price falls to a specified (STOP) level, providing the price has not fallen below a second (LIMIT) level.

PARAMETERS
STOP Trigger Price.

STOP Limit Price.

OBJECTIVE
The objective is to buy at the onset of an uptrend or downtrend, unaffected by market gapping.

MOTIVATION
A STOP order guarantees execution, but not price. It means that a STOP BUY will definitely execute when the specified price is reached, but possibly (though rarely) at an unfavorable price way above the specified price. A STOP SELL will definitely execute when the specified price is

reached, but possibly (though rarely) at an unfavorable price way below the specified price.

This can occur when a price falls or rises rapidly, particularly if the price 'gaps' in overnight trading. That is, if this morning's opening price is significantly higher or lower than the previous day's closing price.

The objective of this order type is therefore to prevent the STOP order from executing in this unfavorable situation.

SUCCESS SCENARIO(s)

In total there are four possible success scenarios for this pattern as follows:

- Our STOP BUY order <u>does execute</u> when the price rises to our STOP price, providing the price has not at the same time risen above our LIMIT price.

- Our STOP BUY order <u>does not execute</u> when the price rises to our STOP price, if the price has at the same time risen above our LIMIT price.

- Our STOP SELL order <u>does execute</u> when the price falls to our STOP price, providing the price has not at the same time fallen below our LIMIT price.

- Our STOP SELL order <u>does not execute</u> when the price falls to our STOP price, and the price has at the same time fallen below our LIMIT price.

The SELL variants of the success scenarios are shown pictorially in Figure 19 and Figure 20.

In Figure 19 we place a STOP / LIMIT SELL order on day 1 when we observe that the price is falling. On day 2 the price falls below our STOP price, but not (at the same time) below our LIMIT price, so the SELL order <u>does execute</u>.

Financial Trading Patterns

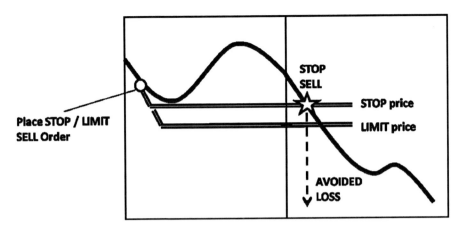

Figure 19 STOP / LIMIT (SELL) success scenario #1

In Figure 19 we place a STOP / LIMIT SELL order on day 1 when we observe that the price is falling. Overnight the price gaps down to open the next day below our STOP price <u>and</u> below our LIMIT price, therefore the SELL order <u>does not execute</u>; which proves to be beneficial because the price rebounds and we need not have sold out at such a low price.

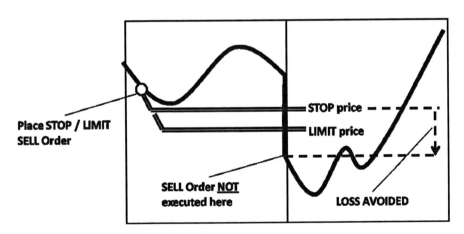

Figure 20 STOP / LIMIT (SELL) success scenario #2

FAILURE SCENARIO(s)

Figure 21 shows a failure for the STOP/LIMIT SELL pattern; in which our STOP SELL order does not execute (because the price falls below our LIMIT) yet the price goes on falling... and falling. With no price rebound to close the gap, we would have been better letting the STOP SELL order execute without a LIMIT.

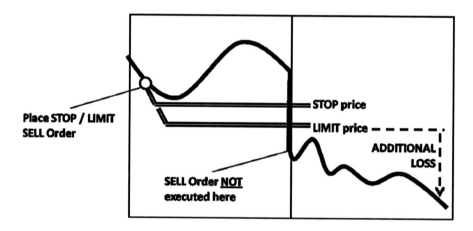

Figure 21 STOP / LIMIT (SELL) failure scenario

Obviously there is a corresponding failure for the STOP/LIMIT BUY pattern; in which we fail to buy-in on an upward price gap, and the price keeps rising ad infinitum. In that failure scenario we would not actually make a loss, but we would be forced to buy-in at an even higher price in future.

APPLICATION

You can apply this pattern only if your stockbroker allows you to place a STOP order with an attached LIMIT, i.e. a STOP/LIMIT order.

Your stockbroker might also provide trailing versions, allowing you to place TRAILING STOP/LIMIT BUY and TRAILING STOP/LIMIT SELL orders.

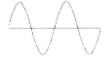

10 – STRADDLE

NAME
STRADDLE

DEFINITIONS
Investopedia (www.investopedia.com) defines a straddle as:

"An options strategy with which the investor holds a position in both a call and put with the same strike price and expiration date."

In plain English: the investor is betting that the price will rise (the CALL) while at the same time betting that the price will fall (the PUT). And while the term 'straddle' is usually defined in terms of 'options', it is possible to establish a straddle on stocks (by buying a stock long, and at the same time selling it short). It is also theoretically possible to establish a straddle using two financial spread bets: a BUY (rising price) bet combined with a SELL (falling price) bet.

PARAMETERS

<u>For Options</u>
CALL Option Strike Price

PUT Option Strike Price

<u>For Stocks, Indexes, or Spread Bets</u>
Long leg STOP SELL Trigger Price

Short leg STOP BUY Trigger Price

OBJECTIVE
The objective is to benefit from high volatility.

MOTIVATION
Investopedia suggests that...

"Straddles are a good strategy to pursue if an investor believes that a stock's price will move significantly, but is unsure as to which direction."

If a specific stock, or the stock market as a whole, suffers a major downward correction we might conclude that:

- It will soon rebound strongly, to recapture the lost ground. What goes down must go back up, right?

- Or, it will keep falling. Obviously there was a good reason for the fall.

Whatever our view, it is unlikely we'll conclude that the price will stay at the current level after a major correction.

So our motivation for this pattern is to benefit if the price rebounds and starts to rise, and also to benefit if the price continues to fall. It sounds like magic, but it isn't. This trick relies on gaining more on the profitable leg of the spread than we lose on the unprofitable leg.

If you're wondering what a 'leg' is, you'll find the answer in the next paragraph.

SUCCESS SCENARIO(s)
A straddle is established by setting up a LONG position (by buying a stock, taking a CALL option, or placing a BUY spread bet) and at the same time setting up a SHORT

position (by selling short a stock, taking a PUT option, or placing a SELL spread bet). Each position, LONG and SHORT, is a 'leg' of the straddle.

If we establish those positions using conventional stocks or spread bets, we must set a STOP order on each leg – to limit the loss on that leg while allowing for maximum gain on the other leg. If we establish the legs using options: the potential loss on each leg will implicitly be limited to our investment on that leg, while the gains on the other leg will be exaggerated thanks to leverage.

The key to the whole pattern, therefore, can be summarized as:

While the losses on one leg will ostensibly cancel out the gains on the other leg, the losses on the losing leg are limited whereas the gains on the winning leg are unlimited – and possibly exaggerated.

In Figure 22, the solid line shows how the price might oscillate (rise and fall) after we establish the spread. The dashed line shows how the value of our long leg (bet on rising price) changes over that time, and the dotted line shows how the value of our short leg (bet on falling price) changes over that time.

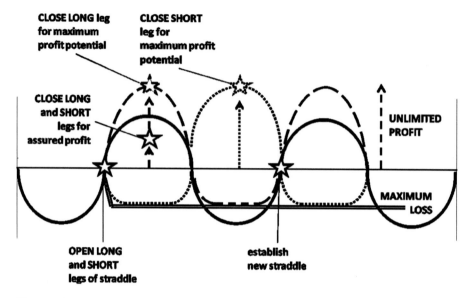

CLOSE LONG leg for maximum profit potential

CLOSE SHORT leg for maximum profit potential

CLOSE LONG and SHORT legs for assured profit

UNLIMITED PROFIT

OPEN LONG and SHORT legs of straddle

establish new straddle

MAXIMUM LOSS

Figure 22 STRADDLE success scenario

The most important thing to notice is that when the price has reached its maximum point:

- The value of our long position has risen by a greater amount, thanks to the leveraged nature of options or spread bets. (The value of our long position would follow the solid price line exactly if we established the long position simply by buying a stock).

- The value of our short position had already fallen to a point of maximum loss, and leveled out; either because we had placed a STOP order, or by the very nature of options.

- The difference between the profit on the long leg (dashed line) and the loss on the short leg (dotted line) is net positive, which means we could close both positions at this time to bank a profit.

If we established the legs of the spread using stocks or spread bets: our stop on the losing leg will have triggered anyway, leaving only the profitable leg to sell.

If we established the legs of the spread using options: both legs will still be in play providing the option expiry dates have not been reached. We could close both positions, as suggested above, or we could adopt a more advanced strategy.

The more advanced strategy would involve closing only the profitable leg ☆, to capture maximum profit on that leg. If the price then swings back the other way (falls significantly), as in Figure 22, the short leg will become profitable and we can close out that leg ☆ also at a profit.

When both positions have been closed we can establish a new straddle if we expect the price volatility to continue.

The other success scenario for this pattern is the one in which the price falls-then-rises rather than rises-than-falls after we establish the legs of the spread. It really makes no difference which way the price moves… as long as the price moves.

FAILURE SCENARIO(s)
The key to the failure scenarios lies in my last statement, "..as long as the price moves".

If we establish a straddle during a period of low volatility, we run the risk that the price will oscillate within the bounds of our maximum loss, as shown in Figure 23.

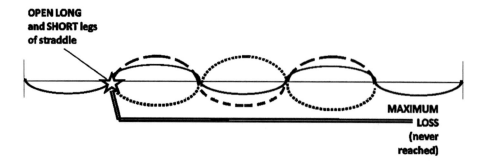

**OPEN LONG
and SHORT legs
of straddle**

**MAXIMUM
LOSS
(never
reached)**

Figure 23 STRADDLE failure scenario

In that failure scenario: at all points, the profit on the winning leg is always offset exactly by the loss on the losing leg. Hence we never have an opportunity to make a net profit.

In the case of a straddle established using stocks or spread bets, we can at least close both positions at any point without actually registering a loss; apart from the transaction charges we paid when opening the positions.

In the case of a straddle established using options, the situation is worse. Any option we take will have a 'strike price' to which the price must rise (for a CALL option) or the price must fall (for a PUT option) before that position is profitable at all. Each option will also have an 'expiry date' by which we must close the position.

As shown in Figure 24: if we reach the expiry date with price having not breached the strike price (upwards) of the CALL option, and the price having not breached the strike price (downwards) of the PUT option, both options will expire worthless.

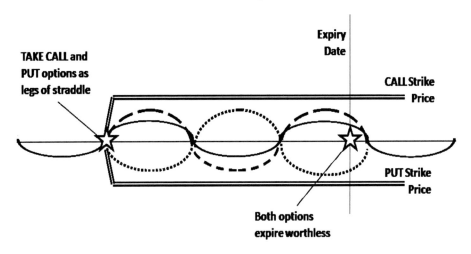

Figure 24 STRADDLE failure scenario (using OPTIONS)

You heard me correctly. If the price does not suffer sufficient volatility, both options could expire worthless; which means we lose all of the money invested on both legs of the straddle!

APPLICATION

As indicated throughout, there are at least three ways to implement this pattern: by buying and short-selling a stock, by simultaneously placing BUY and a SELL spread bet, and – the more usual – taking a CALL and PUT option. Depending on the nature of your stockbroker account(s) you may be able to use one, two, all three, or none of these implementation mechanisms.

Stock Straddle

To implement the pattern as a stock straddle, your stockbroker must allow you to sell stocks short as well as buying stocks long. Not only that; the stockbroker must allow you to buy a stock, short-sell the same stock, and hold both positions open at the same time without the short sell position causing the closure of the long-buy position.

Your stockbroker may well <u>not</u> offer this kind of setup, in which case you'll have to be more creative. One such 'creative' solution would be to hold an account with more than one stockbroker, then establish the long position with one broker and the short position with the other broker (who must at least allow short trading).

Spread Bet Straddle

A 'spread betting' or 'spread trading' account will certainly allow you to trade both ways, long and short, by betting on a falling price as well as on a rising price. Again, it is unlikely that the spread betting provider will allow you to hold long and short positions on the same security simultaneously.

Once again you may need to be creative, by using two separate spread trading accounts to hold the long and short positions. Alternatively, you might place long- and short-bets on different but highly correlated securities. For example, bet long on the Dow Jones 6-month future and bet short on the Dow Jones 3-month future.

Option Straddle

I consider this implementation last because, to be frank, I don't want to delve too deep into options and option theory. Many other good books have been written on that subject. Nonetheless, options are perhaps the most-used implementation mechanism for the STRADDLE pattern.

To use this technique with options, you must have stockbroker account that allows you to buy and sell options or similar derivative instruments (such as *covered warrants* or *contracts for difference*). You might have to jump through some administrative hoops before your stockbroker provides these facilities.

In practice you will find it difficult, if not impossible, to establish a perfect straddle in which both legs (CALL and PUT) have the same expiry date and the same strike price (which coincides with the current market price). You will probably have to settle for a STRANGLE; which is a variation of the pattern in which the expiry dates are the same, and the strike prices are some distance either side of the current market price. Don't forget that you stand to lose your entire investment if the price lands between the two strike prices at expiry date!

Having introduced the STRANGLE pattern in the context of the STRADDLE pattern, it is worth mentioning that both patterns are variants of what is known generically as an 'options spread'. There are myriad other option spreads, with exotic names such as 'butterfly spread', which are characterized by the different – asymmetric – strike prices and expiry dates.

A search of the quoted phrase "option spreads" on your favorite search engine or book-selling web site will point you towards more information on option spreads.

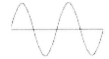

11 – Financial Trading Anti-patterns

In this book about 'patterns', the concept of an 'anti-pattern' might appear to be a little strange. All will become clear as you read on.

Introduction to Anti-patterns

For many years the IT industry had been awash with books documenting tried-and-tested 'patterns' for effective software development. Then one day, someone figured that software developers also routinely applied patterns – that is, structured their code – in ways that were not beneficial at all; maybe even detrimental. That bright spark wrote the first 'anti-patterns' book, describing common ways in which programmers write bad software.

It strikes me that the same thing could apply here. There are many classic traps for the naïve trader to fall in to, as exemplified by the numerous "top 10 stock trading mistakes" books on sale.

I think it would be instructive to rework those classic traps as patterns, or rather anti-patterns, using the same standardized layout and pictorial representations that I've used in this book; but that's for another time.

In the meantime: a good 'exercise for the reader' would be for you to go out and buy one of those 'stock market mistakes' books (I've not written one, sorry) and sketch out what you think the scenario would look like.

I'll get you started...

Sample Anti-pattern Scenarios

By way of demonstration I'll present two sample anti-pattern scenarios here, representing the classic traps of 'holding a falling stock' and 'selling too soon'.

<u>Hold a falling stock</u>

What goes down must come back up, right? Not always, since companies can and do go bust. In the worst case shown in Figure 25, by holding a losing stock we run the risk of losing our entire investment.

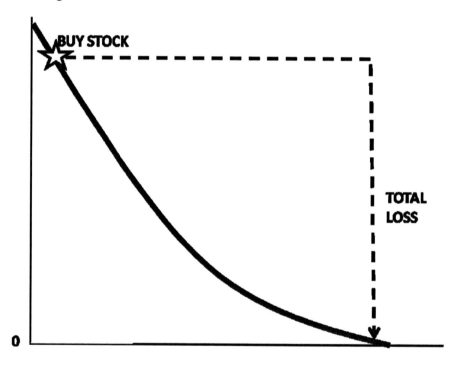

Figure 25 Hold a Falling Stock failure scenario

Even if our 'hold a falling stock' strategy does ultimately result in a profit (Figure 26), we have suffered the opportunity loss of holding an unprofitable position while our money might have been better invested elsewhere.

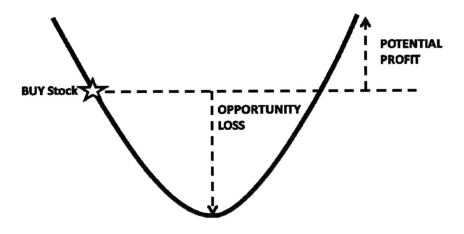

Figure 26 Hold a Falling Stock success scenario

Don't forget that while waiting for the success scenario to play out (Figure 26), we ran the risk of total failure (Figure 25).

Sell too soon

No-one went broke taking a profit, right? Maybe not, but they failed to get as rich as they could.

Figure 27 shows the 'sell too soon' failure scenario in which we take our profit before the stock price realizes its maximum profit potential.

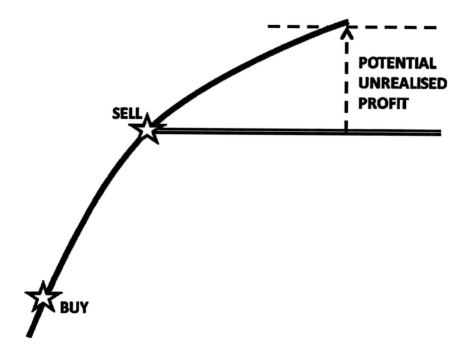

Figure 27 Sell too soon failure scenario

You might recognize this anti-pattern as corresponding with the failure scenario of the LIMIT SELL pattern.

Now, when I agreed that 'no-one went broke taking a profit' I wasn't telling the whole truth. Some people have gone broke by taking profits too soon from profitable positions while holding on to losing trades. After all, a trader will only succeed if the sum of his profits exceeds the sum of his losses; which leads me on to...

Cut the Flowers, Water the Weeds
By combining the anti-patterns 'hold a falling stock' and 'sell too soon' we can conceive a compound anti-pattern named 'cut your profits, let your losses run'; which has been described by a well-known investor as analogous to "cutting the flowers, and watering the weeds".

I'm sure you get the idea now, so I'll let you draw that one.

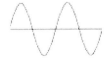

12 – Market Examples

This chapter demonstrates the potential efficacy, or otherwise, of the patterns using real historic price charts. I provide examples of where a particular pattern would have succeeded, and where it would have failed.

These examples are designed to teach some lessons, but you should treat them with a degree of caution. I'll acknowledge in advance that I am guilty of 'confirmation bias', which means that I have chosen price charts specifically to demonstrate my points.

LIMIT BUY, LIMIT SELL

Take a look at Figure 28 which shows the FTSE 100 index price in the period May to October 2007, overlaid with the LIMIT BUY, LIMIT SELL pattern.

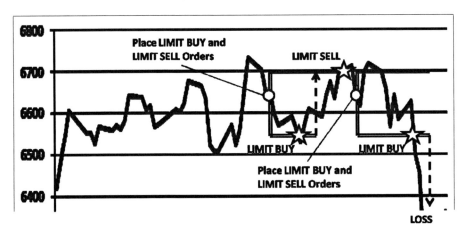

Figure 28 LIMIT BUY, LIMIT SELL on FTSE 100 May to October 2007

I'll now explain the consequence of that sequence of events for the long-only trader and the long-and-short trader.

The Long View

Having observed what he believes to be a trading range, the long-only trader places LIMIT BUY and LIMIT SELL orders, to buy-in near the bottom of the range and sell-out near the top of the range. Sure enough, the LIMIT BUY and LIMIT SELL orders execute as expected and he banks a profit.

Flushed with success, he repeats the setup, but this time with different consequences. The price rises, but the higher (LIMIT SELL) order does not execute because the long-only trader cannot sell something that he doesn't already own. When the price falls again, the LIMIT BUY order executes as expected... but the price continues to fall thus generating a loss; at least on paper.

This real-life sequence of events demonstrates both a success scenario and a failure scenario for a long-only trader employing the LIMIT BUY, LIMIT SELL pattern.

The Long and Short View

Whereas the long-only trader ends up with a loss in this scenario, the long-and-short trader could actually make a profit as follows.

The first LIMIT BUY, LIMIT SELL combination executes exactly as before, generating a profit.

As soon as the second set of LIMIT BUY, LIMIT SELL orders have been placed, the price rises. When the rising price reaches the LIMIT SELL price, that order *can* execute because a long-and-short trader can sell something that she doesn't already own. When the price subsequently falls, the LIMIT BUY order executes to buy back the stock at a lower price. Thus, over the two cycles, she banks double the profit of the long-only trader and is not left holding a paper loss.

TRAILING STOP BUY, TRAILING STOP SELL

Figure 29 shows the Dow Jones Industrial Average (DJIA) index price over the period May 2006 to April 2007, overlaid with the TRAILING STOP BUY, TRAILING STOP SELL pattern.

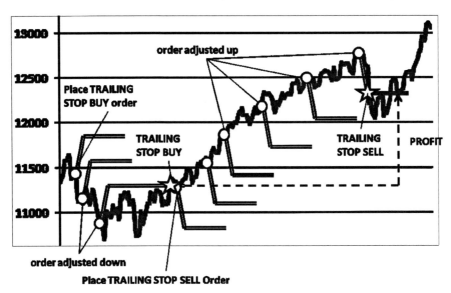

Figure 29 TRAILING STOP BUY, TRAILING STOP SELL on DJIA May 2006 to April 2007

Upon observing a downtrend, we place a TRAILING STOP BUY order that will execute when the trend reverses (price starts to rise). The TRAILING STOP order falls automatically in line with the falling price, such that, when the price does start to rise, we buy-in at a more attractive price than if we had bought-in immediately at the outset.

We then immediately place a TRAILING STOP SELL order, which rises in line with the rising price. The uptrend continues for some time until, when the trend breaks, the

TRAILING STOP SELL executes and we close the position with a healthy profit.

As it happens, we need not have sold out when we did because the uptrend re-establishes taking the price to an even higher level. Don't feel bad about that; at least we held on to most of the gains we had made, and there was nothing to stop us repeating the whole pattern by placing a TRAILING STOP BUY as soon as our TRAILING STOP SELL had executed.

The real problem occurs with this pattern when the price does not trend down, and then trend up, as expected. You can see in Figure 30 what happens when the price simply oscillates. You might recognize the underlying price chart as that used previously in Figure 28 to demonstrate the LIMIT BUY, LIMIT SELL pattern; and whereas in Figure 28 the oscillating price potentially worked to our advantage, in Figure 30 it does not... at least initially.

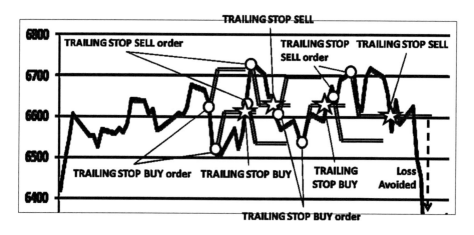

Figure 30 TRAILING STOP BUY, TRAILING STOP SELL on FTSE 100 May to October 2007

Upon observing what we think to be the start of a downtrend, we place a TRAILING STOP BUY order; which adjusts down, and then triggers when the downtrend reverses. We immediately place a TRAILING STOP SELL order; which adjusts up, and then executes when the uptrend reverses.

Do you see what has happened? We sold-out at pretty much the same price that we bought in, having made no real profit once the transaction fees have been accounted for.

Then it repeats.

As soon as the TRAILING STOP SELL executes, we place another TRAILING STOP BUY order to buy-in when the new downtrend reverses. That order executes (buys-in) again at pretty much the same price. We immediately place a TRAILING STOP SELL order, which rises with the price and then subsequently executes (sells-out) at – guess what? – the same price!

We've traded several times in succession, and made no profit, which serves to demonstrate the slight flaw in this pattern: although we avoid big losses, we stand to notch up many small losses (thanks to dealing charges) in a sideways-trading oscillating market. Look out for the big drop at the end of the price chart, though, which we have certainly avoided thanks to the execution of our TRAILING STOP SELL order.

Before we leave this example, I'll hint at how we could have avoided the small 'whipsaw' losses incurred while the price oscillated. One way would be to place the STOP orders at a smaller distance from the current price (so that we profit from even the small oscillations); the other way would be to place the STOP orders at a greater distance from the current prices (so that the orders did not trigger at all until the price moved significantly up or down).

To keep these patterns generic, I have so far conveniently avoided the issue of where to place stop orders in relation to the current price. I haven't ducked the issue entirely, and you'll find my treatment of that issue in chapter *13 – Author's use of Trading Patterns*.

STRADDLE

Figure 31 shows the FTSE 100 index price over the period July 2007 to October 2007, overlaid with the STRADDLE pattern

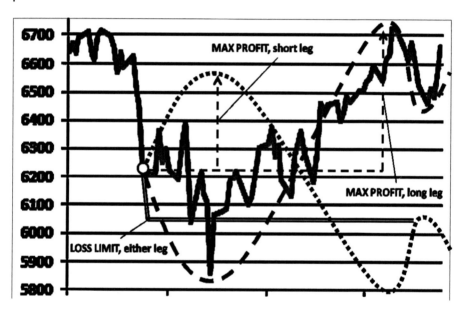

Figure 31 STRADDLE on FTSE100 July 2007 to October 2007

Upon witnessing a notable downward correction, we anticipate a period of high volatility; so we establish a straddle around the 6200 price level. The price oscillates a little, and then falls again significantly, generating a profit on the short leg of the straddle and an opposing loss on the long leg.

Since the loss on the long leg is limited, we have the option of closing out both positions for a net profit. Alternatively we bank the profit on the short leg, and leave open the long position in the hope of a subsequent rebound. Fortunately the price does indeed rebound, allowing us to bank a sizeable profit on the long leg too.

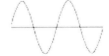

13 – Author's use of Trading Patterns

To show that I'm not superstitious – about the market or anything else for that matter – I've used the number 13 for this chapter dedicated to my own use of trading patterns.

I have applied every one of the patterns in this book while trading on my own account. Although my own biases may have shone through at times, my intention has been to present the patterns dispassionately. That is; to tell you how each pattern works and what it is meant to achieve, without commenting explicitly on the efficacy of each pattern.

The fact is that market conditions change over time, and do not always follow the idealized scenarios shown herein. A pattern that works at one point in time might not work at another point in time. The trick is to learn the patterns, and to determine for yourself how to fit them together in a 'trading system' which works for you in all market conditions.

My own trading system is based on the principle of not losing money, and is documented in my other book "DON'T LOSE MONEY! (in the Stock Markets)", ISBN 978-0-9556-7640-6. That strategy might sound unlikely, but many traders fail to come out with a net profit because the money they make on winning trades is more than offset by the money they make on losing trades.

So which patterns comprise my trading system?

DON'T LOSE MONEY patterns

The following subsections describe the patterns that comprise my DON'T LOSE MONEY trading system.

TRAILING STOP BUY, TRAILING STOP SELL

For regular stock trades and index trades I most often use the TRAILING STOP BUY, TRAILING STOP SELL pattern; to chase a downtrend into a trough before buying in, and to ride an uptrend up to a peak before selling out.

That technique not only helps me to buy low, sell high; but also helps ensure that I DON'T LOSE MONEY, because the TRAILING STOP SELL protects me from any adverse turn of events. Once placed, trailing stops pretty much take care of themselves; so I don't have to watch the market constantly, but I do like to receive an email notification when an order executes.

In sideways-trading, oscillating market conditions I trade often and incur some whipsaw losses. In strongly trending market conditions I trade seldom.

LIMIT BUY, LIMIT SELL

I might consider using the LIMIT BUY, LIMIT SELL pattern in such an oscillating market; but on notification that a LIMIT BUY order has been executed, I must place a STOP SELL at the earliest opportunity to protect against any further fall in price.

STOP BUY, STOP SELL

For spread bets I use the STOP BUY, STOP SELL pattern; which becomes the TRAILING STOP BUY, TRAILING STOP SELL pattern because I trail the stops up and down manually. That is, I adjust the orders myself as I observe the price movements.

In case you're wondering, the reason I don't use an automatic TRAILING STOP is because my spread betting provider doesn't offer one.

STRADDLE / STRANGLE

When trading options (in the guise of covered warrants, or listed contracts for difference) I most often use the STRADDLE, or more accurately the STRANGLE, pattern.

The main reason is that I want some protection (remember, DON'T LOSE MONEY!) but my stockbroker does not provide STOP LOSS protection on options trades. Since options are highly leveraged instruments (you can lose a lot as well as gain a lot) some form of protection is essential.

If I am expecting a period of extreme volatility with the FTSE 100 index sitting at the 6200 level, I will take a CALL option at 6400 and a PUT option at 6000 to establish a STRANGLE. Of course, I'd like to take both options at 6200 (a STRADDLE), but I'm limited to the set of options actually offered through my stockbroker. As the CALL option rises in value, the PUT option falls to compensate, and vice-versa; but whereas the gain on the rising option is theoretically unlimited, the loss on the falling option is limited.

A more advanced strategy would be to combine the STRANGLE pattern with the LIMIT BUY / LIMIT SELL pattern. When I consider the oscillating price to be at a low point I take the CALL option (expecting a rebound upwards), and when I consider the oscillating price to be at a high point I take the PUT option. As a concrete example: I take the 6400 CALL option when the price sits at 6000, then take the 6000 PUT option when the price rises to 6400. At that point the CALL is in profit, and the PUT is not in loss. If the price falls back to 6000 then the PUT will be in profit, and the CALL will not be in loss. At the mid-point 6200, both options will be showing half the profit each.

In this advanced scenario I have secured a profit without having to close the positions. As the price oscillates some more I could buy more 6400 CALLs at 6000 and more 6000 PUTs at 6400, gradually building a large position on each leg of the spread.

The downside to this strategy is that at the outset there will be money invested in only one leg of the spread, with no protection provided by the other leg; which is why it is vitally important to start small. As the positions are built on each leg, any imbalance between the legs will become smaller as a proportion of the overall positions.

Effect of Parameters

The patterns are all well and good, but choosing the right pattern is only half the story. Once you've figured out which pattern to use, you then have to figure out how best to tune the pattern's parameters for greatest effect.

As you saw in Figure 30 of chapter *12 – Market Examples*; by trading the TRAILING STOP BUY, TRAILING STOP SELL pattern against the FTSE 100 in the period May to October 2007, we exposed ourselves to small but frequent 'whipsaw' losses. As I suggested in that chapter, we could avoid those losses by adjusting the trigger distances of the stops. We could make the pattern more effective by adjusting the STOP BUY Trigger Distance and STOP SELL Trigger Distance parameters.

There is no definitive answer to the question of how tight or how wide to set the stop distances. That's a trading Holy Grail if ever there was one. However, I did share my thoughts on that question in my other book, and I'll share them again with you now in brief.

<u>How tight is tight, how wide is wide?</u>
The first thing to bear in mind is the noise, or general variation in prices during the trading day; whereby a price may fall, then rise, then fall by a small amount during the day for no apparent reason. Typically for a major index there might be up to 1% variation in price during the day simply due to this 'noise'.

Usually it makes little sense to set a stop at less than 1% below the current price unless you want to get stopped out for no reason. So in my opinion, a tight stop would be anywhere from 1% below the current price up to about 2% below the current price. I don't want to lose more than 2% on any one trade if I make a wrong call in a down trending market. Remember, don't lose money.

In an upward trending market I will widen my stop initially to about 2.5% below the current price. I say 'initially' because in an upward trending market my aim is to keep the stops as wide as possible, as long as I would stop out at a profit. So once my trade is in profit by a healthy 10% I might be happy to have a 5% stop-point, thus capturing at least half the profit if the tide turns.

Something else to consider is whether there are any apparent support points in the price chart. Investopedia (www.investopedia.com) defines a 'support point' or 'support level' as:

"The price level which, historically, a stock has had difficulty falling below. It is thought of as the level at which a lot of buyers tend to enter the stock."

So rather than setting stops at a percentage below the current price, how about setting stops to coincide with those support points? As each new support point becomes apparent, raise your stop to that new level. Some traders do just that.

14 – Back Testing the Patterns

Question: What does a successful trader do when he thinks he has conceived a new winning trading system?

Answer: He back-tests the system on historic market data.

While past performance is no guarantee of future results, it does help to instill some confidence before committing real money in the live market.

In a sense, back-testing is what I did in chapter *12 – Market Examples*; by overlaying patterns onto real market charts to show how effective they would, or would not, have been in real life. That's a rather manual form of back-testing.

In this chapter I'll investigate how we could set about automating the back-testing of the patterns.

To automate the back-testing we need:

- A pattern that can be automated because it depends on objective price action rather than on subjective value judgments.

- A source of historic market price data.

- A computer program.

- A facility for analyzing the results.

Let's take each of those in turn.

Choice of Pattern

In this example I'll choose to back-test the TRAILING STOP BUY, TRAILING STOP SELL pattern. It is one of the more interesting patterns, and it lends itself to back-testing. Why? Because the buy and sell decisions are based solely on objective price action rather than subjective value judgments.

Obtaining Historic Data

A popular provider of historic market data for the purpose of back-testing is Yahoo! Finance. Visit the Yahoo! Finance page at http://finance.yahoo.com/, navigate to the page for the stock or index you're interested in, and click the Historical Prices link as shown in Figure 32.

Figure 32 Yahoo! Finance DJI page with Historical Prices link

That will take you to the Historical Prices page (Figure 33), which allows you to select a date range for the dataset you want.

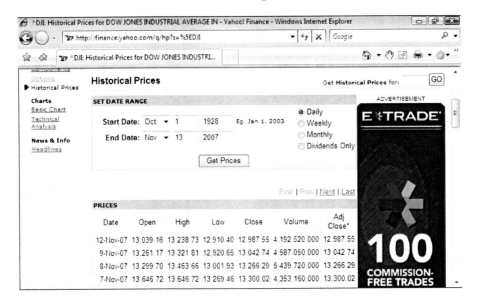

Figure 33 Yahoo! Finance Historical Prices page

Lower down the page (not shown) there is hyperlink labeled *Download To Spreadsheet*, which saves the dataset to your computer as a comma-separated-values (.csv) file.

By default the file will have a name such as `table.csv`, and when opened using Windows Notepad the contents of the file look like this:

```
Date,Open,High,Low,Close,Volume,Adj Close

2007-10-26,13675.66,13885.95,13622.01,13806.70,3612120000,13806.70

2007-10-25,13677.85,13819.78,13471.87,13671.92,4183960000,13671.92

2007-10-24,13675.58,13751.50,13423.74,13675.25,4003300000,13675.25

2007-10-23,13568.93,13754.91,13494.95,13676.23,3309120000,13676.23

2007-10-22,13521.62,13636.80,13337.90,13566.97,3471830000,13566.97

2007-10-19,13888.47,13888.47,13478.94,13522.02,4160970000,13522.02

2007-10-18,13887.90,13984.39,13746.22,13888.96,3203210000,13888.96
```

Alternatively you can open the file in Microsoft Excel like this:

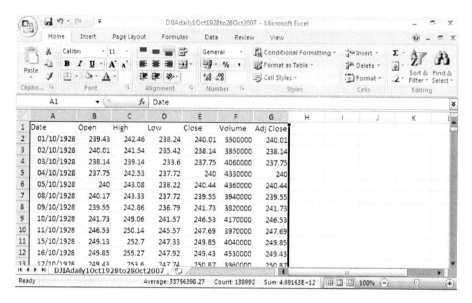

Figure 34 DJI Historic Data

Before opening the file I gave it a more meaningful name of `DJIAdaily1Oct1928to28Oct2007.csv`, and after opening the file I used Excel's sorting feature to sort the data oldest-to-newest. That sorting will be important when I come to run the test program; because I want it to trade the market in the right direction.

Writing the Computer Program

If you're interested the idea of back-testing your trading strategies, if you have little or no aptitude for computer programming, and if you're willing to invest some money in this endeavor, then you could take a look at one of the pre-written all-in-one strategy-testing computer applications such as TradeStation (www.tradestation.com).

If you have some programming ability, you could consider implementing the back-testing computer program as a Microsoft Excel macro. With the source data already in Excel (previous section) and with the prospect of using Excel to analyze the results (next section), that route is an appealing.

For my example, I chose to write a program in Visual Basic .NET, using Microsoft's free Visual Basic Express development environment that you can find at http://msdn.microsoft.com/vstudio/express/.

I don't want to turn this in to a programming tutorial, so I won't go into detail about exactly how I used the development environment to create my program. Those of you with a software development background will have your own ideas about how to do it, and the rest of you probably only want to see the results.

I will summarize the trading rules that the program implements.

1. Trail the market down until it reverses (turns up) as far as the TRAILING STOP BUY Trigger Distance.

2. Buy into the market at that price, using all available funds.

3. Trail the market price up until it reverses (turns down) as far as the TRAILING STOP SELL Trigger Distance.

4. Sell out at that price, and bank the proceeds.

5. Return to step 1.

Some subtleties that you should be aware of are:

- We can only hold one position at a time, with all available funds invested.

- If step 4 results in a profit, we'll have more funds available to invest next time around; if step 4 results in a loss we'll have fewer funds available to invest next time around.

- The TRAILING STOP BUY Trigger Distance and TRAILING STOP SELL Trigger Distance are fixed during the program run, but may be varied for each run.

Analyzing the Results

For the initial test run I used a dataset comprising the historic FTSE100 index closing prices from 2 April 1984 to 28 October 2007. I set the TRAILING STOP BUY Trigger Distance to trail 1% above the falling price, and the TRAILING STOP SELL Trigger Distance to trail 10% below the rising price.

Program Transcript

I have listed the transcript from the back-testing program below. As you scan the transcript, look out for:

- How the `targetBuy` price trails consistently 1% above the falling price.

- How we buy-in (`Invest`) using whatever cash funds are available at the time, initial 1000 (dollars, pounds, Euros, or whatever we choose).

- How the `targetSell` price trails consistently 10% below the rising price.

- How we sell-out (`SELL`), retaining whatever funds we have accumulated to invest in the next cycle.

For brevity I present only the first buy-sell-buy cycle here, followed by the final closeout values. You can find the complete transcript in **Appendix B – Back Testing Transcript**.

Financial Trading Patterns

```
08/06/1984 1068 : targetBuy @ 1079
21/06/1984 1041 : targetBuy @ 1051
27/06/1984 1037 : targetBuy @ 1047
05/07/1984 1061 : Invest 1000 at 1061
17/08/1984 1077 : targetSell @ 969
09/10/1984 1138 : targetSell @ 1024
07/12/1984 1185 : targetSell @ 1066
11/12/1984 1200 : targetSell @ 1080
23/01/1985 1283 : targetSell @ 1155
25/01/1985 1284 : targetSell @ 1156
12/03/1985 1300 : targetSell @ 1170
17/04/1985 1304 : targetSell @ 1174
13/05/1985 1333 : targetSell @ 1200
01/11/1985 1379 : targetSell @ 1241
06/11/1985 1395 : targetSell @ 1256
22/11/1985 1451 : targetSell @ 1306
12/02/1986 1470 : targetSell @ 1323
21/02/1986 1518 : targetSell @ 1366
24/02/1986 1533 : targetSell @ 1380
01/04/1986 1684 : targetSell @ 1516
07/01/1987 1722 : targetSell @ 1550
09/01/1987 1752 : targetSell @ 1577
28/01/1987 1812 : targetSell @ 1631
10/02/1987 1875 : targetSell @ 1688
18/02/1987 1952 : targetSell @ 1757
26/02/1987 1980 : targetSell @ 1782
13/03/1987 2000 : targetSell @ 1800
23/03/1987 2033 : targetSell @ 1830
14/05/1987 2180 : targetSell @ 1962
29/05/1987 2203 : targetSell @ 1983
16/06/1987 2309 : targetSell @ 2078
06/07/1987 2352 : targetSell @ 2117
09/07/1987 2371 : targetSell @ 2134
14/07/1987 2403 : targetSell @ 2163
29/10/1987 1682 : SELL at 1682, cash=1585
15/12/1987 1670 : targetBuy @ 1687
18/12/1987 1717 : Invest 1585 at 1717
...
FINAL SELL at 6482, cash=7015
```

The end result of applying the TRAILING STOP BUY, TRAILING STOP SELL pattern over that time period is to turn a 1000 initial cash balance into a 7015 final cash balance over 23 years.

In addition to providing a transcript (above), my program also writes an output file containing an entry for every day of the time period. Each daily entry gives the date, that day's market price and the value of our holdings at that point as follows:

```
...
20/07/1984,1009,951
06/08/1984,1058,997
17/08/1984,1077,1015
09/10/1984,1138,1073
10/10/1984,1137,1072
18/10/1984,1090,1027
07/12/1984,1185,1117
11/12/1984,1200,1131
23/01/1985,1283,1209
25/01/1985,1284,1210
...
```

As a comma-separated-values (.csv) file I can import it directly into Microsoft Excel, just as I could with the original source data file. And once in Excel, I can very easily generate a chart like the one shown in Figure 35.

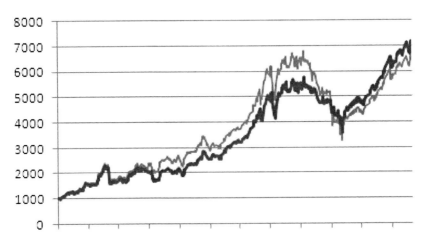

Figure 35 TRAILING STOP BUY, TRAILING STOP SELL – 2 April 1984 to 28 October 2007

The thinner line represents the changing index price over the time period, and the thicker line shows the value of our holdings (in cash, or fully invested) over the same period.

Although our final cash value of 7015 beats the final index value of 6482, you can see from the chart what a close-run thing it was. You can also see that for a significant period of time we underperformed. It all goes to show that – over the long term – the 'buy and hold' folks have probably got it right.

Effect of different time periods

But wait! Look at Figure 36 to see how things would have turned out over the time period 4 January 1999 to 28 October 2007. Remember that the thinner line represents the market price and the thicker line represents the value of our holdings.

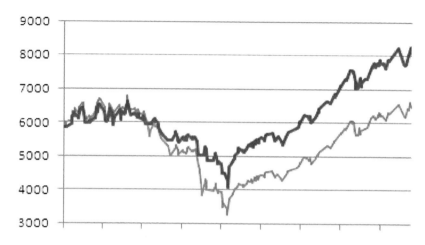

Figure 36 TRAILING STOP BUY, TRAILING STOP SELL – 04 January 1999 to 28 October 2007

The final values are 8095 (our holdings) vs. 6482 (the index), so we have in that case exceeded the potential buy-and-hold returns by almost 25%.

Effect of varying parameters
While you can alter the time period for back-testing purposes, to see how the pattern performs under various market conditions, you can't do that in real trading. When trading for real, you're in whatever time period you find yourself in; no choice.

What you can alter retrospectively (for back testing) or prospectively (for live trading) are the parameter value settings. For the original back tests I set the TRAILING STOP BUY Trigger Distance to 1% and the TRAILING STOP SELL Trigger Distance to 10%. Now I rerun the back-tests with a TRAILING STOP BUY Trigger Distance of 20% and a TRAILING STOP SELL Trigger Distance to 10%.

Figure 37 shows the effect of those new parameter settings over the time period 4 January 1999 to 28 October 2007.

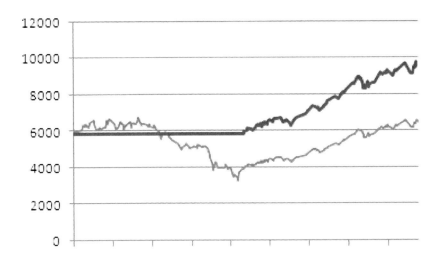

Figure 37 TRAILING STOP BUY, TRAILING STOP SELL – 04 January 1999 to 28 October 2007

The final value of our holdings in that case is 9588, compared with a final index value of 6482, and compared with a final value of 8095 using the original parameter values. And notice that for some time the value of our holdings did not fall in line with the falling price.

Looks promising, eh?

Now take a look at Figure 38, which shows the performance with the new parameter settings over the original time period 2 April 1984 to 28 September 2007.

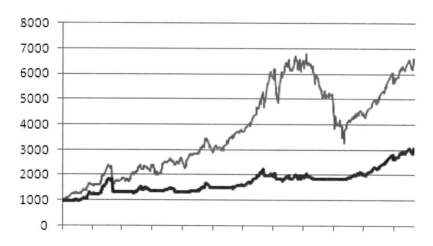

Figure 38 TRAILING STOP BUY, TRAILING STOP SELL – 2 April 1984 to 28 October 2007

In that case our final holding value of 3010 compares very unfavorably with the final index value of 6482. So there's no sure thing in the stock market, after all.

Final Thoughts

In this book I have illustrated that there are several ways to 'trade' utilizing specific stockbroker order types, or combinations thereof.

I've suggested that different patterns might suit different market conditions (chapter *12 – Market Examples*). I've also demonstrated that choosing the right pattern to trade is only half the battle. You need to also get values of the parameters just right (chapter *13 – Author's use of Trading Patterns* and this chapter).

Is it any wonder then, that the majority of stock market traders are not successful?

But you won't let that put you off, will you?

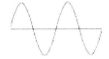

Appendix A – Glossary of Order Types

This appendix provides a non-exhaustive glossary of the stockbroker order types used to implement the patterns in this book.

Unconditional Order Types
The following unconditional orders execute as soon as possible after you have authorized them.

Quote
A 'quote' or 'quote and deal' order gives you the real-time price from the market, and holds that price for you for a few seconds while you decide whether to deal.

At Best
An 'at best' order ensures that your order is executed as soon as possible, at the prevailing market price.

Conditional Order Types
The following conditional orders sit with your broker until a specific condition, such as a fall in price, triggers their execution.

Limit
A 'limit' order executes when the market price is more favorable than the current price; i.e. when the price falls to a

desired level (for a 'limit buy' order), or when the price rises to a desired level (for a 'limit sell' order).

A limit order guarantees price but not execution.

See LIMIT BUY and LIMIT SELL patterns.

Stop
A 'stop' order executes when the market price moves up (for a 'stop buy' order) or down (for a 'stop sell' order); allowing you to buy-in to an uptrend, and sell-out of a downtrend.

A stop order aims to secure execution (if the condition is met) but not price (which may be unfavorable due to slippage). A 'guaranteed stop' order guarantees the execution price.

See STOP BUY and STOP SELL patterns.

Stop with Limit
A 'stop with limit' order executes when the market price moves up (for a 'stop buy' order) or down (for a 'stop sell' order), providing the price movement has not exceeded a limit that you set.

See STOP / LIMIT pattern.

Trailing Stop
A 'trailing stop' order tracks the market price and executes when the price trend reverses by a specified amount. You may also be able to place a limit on a trailing stop order, to give a 'trailing stop with limit'.

See TRAILING STOP BUY and TRAILING STOP SELL patterns.

Order Time Limits

When you place an order, you might also specify a time limit. The order may be executed at any time up to that time limit (if the trigger condition is met), and will be cancelled once the time limit has been reached.

The time limit may be specified as a number of days from one to 30 (or more, if your stockbroker allows) or may be specified in shorthand form. Some of the common shorthand forms are as follows:

GTC, Good 'Till Cancelled: there is no time limit on the order, unless the broker places an overall mandatory time limit.

GFD, Good For Day (or 'Day Order'): the order will be cancelled if not executed the same day.

GTW, Good This Week: the order will be cancelled if not executed in the current week.

GTM, Good This Month: the order will be cancelled if not executed in the current month.

Other Order Types and Time Limits

Your stockbroker may well offer other order types, time limits and combinations that are beyond the scope of this book. An example would be:

One Cancels Other (OCO): which allows you to specify that the execution of one order causes the cancellation of another order.

By utilizing these more exotic order types you can apply ever more exotic patterns.

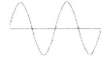

Appendix B – Back Testing Transcript

This appendix lists the complete transcript from the back testing example referred to in chapter **14 – Back Testing the Patterns**. To keep the transcript shorter than the six-thousand-or-so daily entries in the source data, I have listed only the significant events including:

- Price changes that trigger a BUT or SELL order to execute.

- Price changes that cause the trailing stops to move up or down in line with the price.

```
08/06/1984 1068 : targetBuy @ 1079
21/06/1984 1041 : targetBuy @ 1051
27/06/1984 1037 : targetBuy @ 1047
05/07/1984 1061 : Invest 1000 at 1061
17/08/1984 1077 : targetSell @ 969
09/10/1984 1138 : targetSell @ 1024
07/12/1984 1185 : targetSell @ 1066
11/12/1984 1200 : targetSell @ 1080
23/01/1985 1283 : targetSell @ 1155
25/01/1985 1284 : targetSell @ 1156
12/03/1985 1300 : targetSell @ 1170
17/04/1985 1304 : targetSell @ 1174
13/05/1985 1333 : targetSell @ 1200
01/11/1985 1379 : targetSell @ 1241
06/11/1985 1395 : targetSell @ 1256
22/11/1985 1451 : targetSell @ 1306
12/02/1986 1470 : targetSell @ 1323
```

```
21/02/1986 1518 : targetSell @ 1366
24/02/1986 1533 : targetSell @ 1380
01/04/1986 1684 : targetSell @ 1516
07/01/1987 1722 : targetSell @ 1550
09/01/1987 1752 : targetSell @ 1577
28/01/1987 1812 : targetSell @ 1631
10/02/1987 1875 : targetSell @ 1688
18/02/1987 1952 : targetSell @ 1757
26/02/1987 1980 : targetSell @ 1782
13/03/1987 2000 : targetSell @ 1800
23/03/1987 2033 : targetSell @ 1830
14/05/1987 2180 : targetSell @ 1962
29/05/1987 2203 : targetSell @ 1983
16/06/1987 2309 : targetSell @ 2078
06/07/1987 2352 : targetSell @ 2117
09/07/1987 2371 : targetSell @ 2134
14/07/1987 2403 : targetSell @ 2163
29/10/1987 1682 : SELL at 1682, cash=1585
15/12/1987 1670 : targetBuy @ 1687
18/12/1987 1717 : Invest 1585 at 1717
18/01/1988 1790 : targetSell @ 1611
08/03/1988 1815 : targetSell @ 1634
20/06/1988 1844 : targetSell @ 1660
04/07/1988 1848 : targetSell @ 1663
06/07/1988 1870 : targetSell @ 1683
08/08/1988 1876 : targetSell @ 1688
25/01/1989 1939 : targetSell @ 1745
21/02/1989 2061 : targetSell @ 1855
13/03/1989 2103 : targetSell @ 1893
28/04/1989 2118 : targetSell @ 1906
04/05/1989 2119 : targetSell @ 1907
22/05/1989 2169 : targetSell @ 1952
22/06/1989 2180 : targetSell @ 1962
29/06/1989 2182 : targetSell @ 1964
13/07/1989 2258 : targetSell @ 2032
21/07/1989 2283 : targetSell @ 2055
28/07/1989 2306 : targetSell @ 2075
17/08/1989 2360 : targetSell @ 2124
05/09/1989 2426 : targetSell @ 2183
08/05/1990 2182 : SELL at 2182, cash=2014
10/05/1990 2157 : targetBuy @ 2179
```

Financial Trading Patterns

```
04/06/1990 2379 : Invest 2014 at 2379
14/06/1990 2403 : targetSell @ 2163
17/07/1990 2415 : targetSell @ 2174
23/08/1990 2075 : SELL at 2075, cash=1757
04/09/1990 2148 : Invest 1757 at 2148
05/02/1991 2202 : targetSell @ 1982
11/02/1991 2279 : targetSell @ 2051
27/02/1991 2348 : targetSell @ 2113
08/03/1991 2455 : targetSell @ 2210
19/03/1991 2459 : targetSell @ 2213
17/04/1991 2545 : targetSell @ 2290
17/07/1991 2561 : targetSell @ 2305
29/07/1991 2595 : targetSell @ 2336
16/08/1991 2621 : targetSell @ 2359
22/08/1991 2623 : targetSell @ 2361
03/09/1991 2669 : targetSell @ 2402
10/12/1991 2392 : SELL at 2392, cash=1957
30/12/1991 2420 : Invest 1957 at 2420
22/01/1992 2522 : targetSell @ 2270
28/01/1992 2552 : targetSell @ 2297
26/02/1992 2565 : targetSell @ 2308
13/04/1992 2591 : targetSell @ 2332
24/04/1992 2643 : targetSell @ 2379
28/04/1992 2651 : targetSell @ 2386
21/05/1992 2702 : targetSell @ 2432
22/05/1992 2715 : targetSell @ 2444
27/07/1992 2348 : SELL at 2348, cash=1899
13/08/1992 2318 : targetBuy @ 2341
25/08/1992 2281 : targetBuy @ 2304
02/09/1992 2313 : Invest 1899 at 2313
15/09/1992 2370 : targetSell @ 2133
18/09/1992 2567 : targetSell @ 2310
22/09/1992 2586 : targetSell @ 2327
25/09/1992 2601 : targetSell @ 2341
20/10/1992 2617 : targetSell @ 2355
18/11/1992 2704 : targetSell @ 2434
01/12/1992 2792 : targetSell @ 2513
22/12/1992 2842 : targetSell @ 2558
08/02/1993 2870 : targetSell @ 2583
16/06/1993 2883 : targetSell @ 2595
28/06/1993 2897 : targetSell @ 2607
```

```
30/06/1993 2900 : targetSell @ 2610
03/08/1993 2945 : targetSell @ 2650
17/08/1993 3025 : targetSell @ 2722
23/08/1993 3042 : targetSell @ 2738
31/08/1993 3100 : targetSell @ 2790
22/10/1993 3199 : targetSell @ 2879
29/12/1993 3462 : targetSell @ 3116
20/01/1994 3470 : targetSell @ 3123
03/05/1994 3100 : SELL at 3100, cash=2545
28/06/1994 2909 : targetBuy @ 2938
05/07/1994 2965 : Invest 2545 at 2965
18/07/1994 3082 : targetSell @ 2774
10/08/1994 3167 : targetSell @ 2850
08/09/1994 3180 : targetSell @ 2862
19/05/1995 3261 : targetSell @ 2935
02/06/1995 3345 : targetSell @ 3010
06/06/1995 3380 : targetSell @ 3042
10/07/1995 3455 : targetSell @ 3110
11/07/1995 3464 : targetSell @ 3118
24/08/1995 3520 : targetSell @ 3168
13/10/1995 3568 : targetSell @ 3211
18/10/1995 3593 : targetSell @ 3234
24/11/1995 3624 : targetSell @ 3262
27/11/1995 3649 : targetSell @ 3284
23/01/1996 3735 : targetSell @ 3362
14/02/1996 3745 : targetSell @ 3370
23/04/1996 3833 : targetSell @ 3450
29/08/1996 3885 : targetSell @ 3496
06/09/1996 3893 : targetSell @ 3504
03/10/1996 4000 : targetSell @ 3600
29/11/1996 4058 : targetSell @ 3652
27/12/1996 4091 : targetSell @ 3682
20/01/1997 4194 : targetSell @ 3775
27/01/1997 4212 : targetSell @ 3791
14/02/1997 4341 : targetSell @ 3907
30/04/1997 4436 : targetSell @ 3992
01/05/1997 4445 : targetSell @ 4000
13/05/1997 4691 : targetSell @ 4222
17/07/1997 4949 : targetSell @ 4454
21/08/1997 4978 : targetSell @ 4480
06/10/1997 5300 : targetSell @ 4770
```

Financial Trading Patterns

```
13/11/1997 4711 : SELL at 4711, cash=4044
17/11/1997 4867 : Invest 4044 at 4867
27/11/1997 4889 : targetSell @ 4400
02/02/1998 5599 : targetSell @ 5039
24/02/1998 5651 : targetSell @ 5086
23/03/1998 5947 : targetSell @ 5352
07/04/1998 6094 : targetSell @ 5485
17/07/1998 6174 : targetSell @ 5557
20/07/1998 6179 : targetSell @ 5561
14/08/1998 5455 : SELL at 5455, cash=4533
04/09/1998 5167 : targetBuy @ 5219
07/09/1998 5347 : Invest 4533 at 5347
06/11/1998 5491 : targetSell @ 4942
11/01/1999 6085 : targetSell @ 5476
25/03/1999 6085 : targetSell @ 5476
01/04/1999 6330 : targetSell @ 5697
23/04/1999 6428 : targetSell @ 5785
09/06/1999 6453 : targetSell @ 5808
05/07/1999 6592 : targetSell @ 5933
01/12/1999 6646 : targetSell @ 5981
06/12/1999 6694 : targetSell @ 6025
01/09/2000 6795 : targetSell @ 6116
19/02/2001 6094 : SELL at 6094, cash=5166
06/03/2001 6012 : targetBuy @ 6072
28/03/2001 5614 : targetBuy @ 5670
10/04/2001 5803 : Invest 5166 at 5803
01/05/2001 5928 : targetSell @ 5335
10/05/2001 5964 : targetSell @ 5368
31/08/2001 5345 : SELL at 5345, cash=4758
05/09/2001 5316 : targetBuy @ 5369
05/10/2001 5036 : targetBuy @ 5086
18/10/2001 5116 : Invest 4758 at 5116
16/11/2001 5291 : targetSell @ 4762
19/11/2001 5338 : targetSell @ 4804
18/06/2002 4702 : SELL at 4702, cash=4373
25/06/2002 4631 : targetBuy @ 4677
26/06/2002 4531 : targetBuy @ 4576
11/07/2002 4230 : targetBuy @ 4272
23/07/2002 3858 : targetBuy @ 3897
06/08/2002 4131 : Invest 4373 at 4131
16/08/2002 4330 : targetSell @ 3897
```

```
22/01/2003 3678 : SELL at 3678, cash=3893
28/01/2003 3490 : targetBuy @ 3525
06/02/2003 3597 : Invest 3893 at 3597
25/03/2003 3762 : targetSell @ 3386
24/04/2003 3899 : targetSell @ 3509
30/04/2003 3926 : targetSell @ 3533
14/05/2003 3975 : targetSell @ 3578
16/05/2003 4049 : targetSell @ 3644
10/06/2003 4113 : targetSell @ 3702
18/06/2003 4207 : targetSell @ 3786
16/09/2003 4299 : targetSell @ 3869
10/10/2003 4311 : targetSell @ 3880
17/10/2003 4344 : targetSell @ 3910
13/11/2003 4373 : targetSell @ 3936
14/11/2003 4397 : targetSell @ 3957
01/12/2003 4410 : targetSell @ 3969
22/12/2003 4424 : targetSell @ 3982
07/01/2004 4473 : targetSell @ 4026
20/02/2004 4515 : targetSell @ 4064
01/03/2004 4537 : targetSell @ 4083
09/03/2004 4542 : targetSell @ 4088
20/04/2004 4569 : targetSell @ 4112
23/04/2004 4570 : targetSell @ 4113
17/09/2004 4591 : targetSell @ 4132
10/12/2004 4694 : targetSell @ 4225
21/12/2004 4733 : targetSell @ 4260
04/01/2005 4847 : targetSell @ 4362
10/02/2005 5000 : targetSell @ 4500
01/06/2005 5011 : targetSell @ 4510
16/06/2005 5045 : targetSell @ 4540
20/06/2005 5072 : targetSell @ 4565
24/06/2005 5079 : targetSell @ 4571
01/07/2005 5161 : targetSell @ 4645
13/09/2005 5338 : targetSell @ 4804
14/11/2005 5470 : targetSell @ 4923
24/11/2005 5511 : targetSell @ 4960
22/12/2005 5597 : targetSell @ 5037
13/01/2006 5711 : targetSell @ 5140
20/02/2006 5863 : targetSell @ 5277
10/04/2006 6067 : targetSell @ 5460
19/10/2006 6156 : targetSell @ 5540
```

Financial Trading Patterns

```
07/11/2006 6244 : targetSell @ 5620
15/12/2006 6260 : targetSell @ 5634
03/01/2007 6319 : targetSell @ 5687
21/06/2007 6596 : targetSell @ 5936
10/10/2007 6633 : targetSell @ 5970
FINAL SELL at 6482, cash=7015
```

Also by This Author

Tony Loton's trading & finance books are available from the LOTON*tech* online store at http://stores.lulu.com/lotontech.

If your investment falls by 50% you'll need a 100% rise just to get you back where you started. So when speculating in the markets, protecting the money you do have is just as important as making some more. This book is for you if you'd like to have a go at beating the system, but don't want to lose your shirt in the process. Topics covered include: index investing, market timing and trend following, stop loss orders, position sizing, straddles and strangles.

"I found it very easy to understand, not too much jargon..."

"I rather enjoyed the experience notes at the end of each chapter..."

ISBN: 978-0-9556764-0-6

Table of Figures

Index

Lightning Source UK Ltd.
Milton Keynes UK
27 November 2009

146770UK00002B/159/P